A MINDSET GUIDE FOR

EVERY YOUNG SPORTS PLAYER

I0559442

DEVELOP
A
WINNERS
MIND

WINNER'S MIND SERIES BOOK 1

CHRIS DAWSON

with
Niki the Mind Coach

MALCHIK MEDIA

A Malchik Media &
www.richardlynttonbooks.com publication

Cover design by Elisabetta Giordana

Interior design by Gary A. Rosenberg • thebookcouple.com

For Grace and Taylor,
Two aspiring young sports people

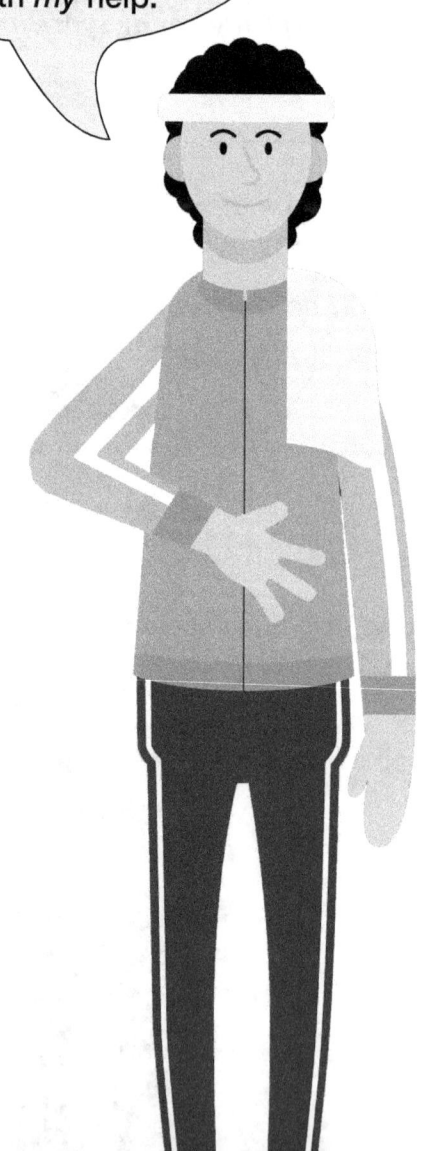

"Winning isn't everything, but striving to win is."

—Vince Lombardi
Head Coach of Green Bay Packers
(American Football team)

Foreword

Paul Lake, Manchester City F.C.
and England Under 21s

I've devoted my whole life to football. I played professionally for Manchester City, worked as a qualified physiotherapist across all professional divisions, and gained a vast amount of experience working for the Premier League in support of children, young adults, and staff within the professional game.

Having read *Develop a Winner's Mind*, I believe this book should be the ultimate guide for every young person and parent as they embark on the journey into the exciting world of team sports. The tips, tools, and techniques are easy to follow, can be used at any time, and could be extremely effective as you strive to be the best version of yourself.

The book is full of quotes from amazing people in sport, who have developed their own unique ways of winning, of dealing with setbacks, and all without losing their love of sport.

It highlights the importance of training our minds as well as our bodies, to recognise that how we feel affects how we think and behave, and that there is success in losing, not just in winning.

Essentially, being human and loving ourselves, is the most important first step.

Introduction

Sport is played with the body.

But the mind must be in gear.

Yes, having a fit mind is as important as a fit body and, like the body, the mind has to be encouraged and trained to perform at its best.

This book is an introduction to the mental aspects of sport and is aimed at young people aged 12 years old and upwards. However, anyone coming to this topic for the first time, will pick up useful hints about the mind game. Adopting just a few of the ideas in this book will raise your game, whatever your age, whatever your sport.

Although mental skills apply to all sports, you will notice that this book mostly approaches the topic from the angle of ball games and team games, rather than individual sports like athletics or skateboarding.

Even so, the same approaches apply to these sports—for example, being able to be calm and relaxed, developing a "can do" mindset and taking practice seriously.

Good luck and good luck with your mental training!

—Chris and Niki

Whatever sport you play, this book is for you.

Which sport(s) do you play?

Write it next to the appropriate letter. Can you name a sport for each letter?

A _____   N _____

B _____   O _____

C _____   P _____

D _____   Q _____

E _____   R _____

F _____   S _____

G _____   T _____

H _____   U _____

I _____   V _____

J _____   W _____

K _____   X _____

L _____   Y _____

M _____   Z _____

Were you able to think of a sport for the letters X and Z? (See pages 41 & 45.)

Always remember:

It's OK to love playing sport.

It's OK to love competing.

But above all, it's most important to love yourself.

Win or lose, you are still you, and OK just as you are.

"What's your best discovery?" asked the mole.
"That I'm enough as I am," said the boy.
—CHARLIE MACKESY, AUTHOR OF *THE BOY,*
THE MOLE, THE FOX AND THE HORSE

Take Your Time

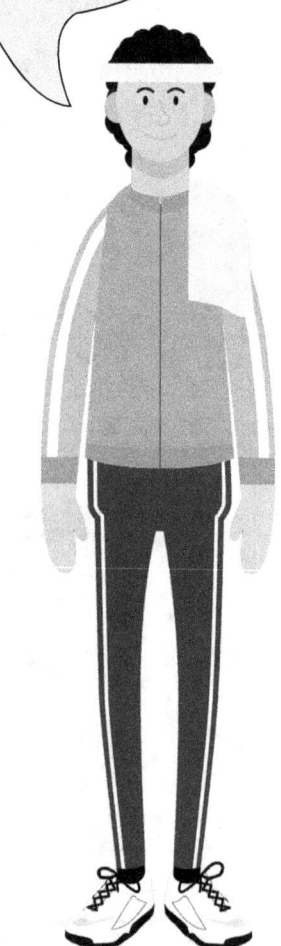

If something doesn't help you yet—it's OK. It may be of help later.

There's lots to take in about the mental game. So it's OK to read a bit of this booklet at a time, to let it sink in and to go away and try it out. You can always come back to it later. See what works for you.

Good luck!

Developing your brain game is as important as developing your physical skills.

A positive attitude helps. So, let's start with a "Can Do" attitude.

Henry Ford—yes, the one who built cars—famously said,

> *"If you think you can do a thing, or think you can't do a thing, you are probably right."*

Do you think you can?

Yes you can.
With my help.
So have a go!

Feelings, Thoughts, and Actions

What you are *feeling* affects how you are *thinking,* and how you are *thinking* affects how you *play.*

Does that sound a bit complicated?

Let's take an example.

> You feel *tired* before you play. You start thinking how *hard* it's going to be to play today. You start the game slowly and without much energy. And then what happens? Yes, you don't play very well, and you get a bit fed up with yourself and so it goes on—unless you break the cycle.

Imagine the opposite.

> You are feeling awake and full of energy. You can't wait to play. Your thoughts are about playing well and enjoying the game. Mind and body feel positive and ready, and you set up a positive cycle.

> *"The person who can control their state can control their world."*
>
> —TIGER WOODS, WINNER OF 15 MAJOR
> GOLF CHAMPIONSHIPS & 81 PGA TOURS.

So, let's learn to be ready to play. To train mind and body to be in the best state to play your favourite sport.

When things don't go to plan— and quite often they don't— you have two choices:

✗ You can moan, groan, complain, give up ...

　OR

✔ Be upset for a moment

✔ Express your feelings

✔ Talk about it

✔ Learn from what has happened

And, as the song goes:

"Pick yourself up,
Dust yourself off,
Start all over again."

It's called "Developing a Growth Mindset."

It takes practice.
Keep giving it a go.
It's worth it!

Success Comes Out of Setbacks

A couple of thoughts from people who have been there:

"Believe in yourself and don't be afraid of making mistakes, because mistakes are part of your growth. Mistakes don't mean you are not good enough. It means you are evolving. You will become the best version of yourself."

—SARINA WIEGMAN, MANAGER OF ENGLAND WOMEN'S FOOTBALL (SOCCER) TEAM, WINNERS OF THE 2022 EUROPEAN CHAMPIONSHIPS AND RUNNERS UP IN THE 2023 WORLD CHAMPIONSHIPS

"Winning does not happen in a straight line . . . In order to win you have to know how to lose. You have to know how to handle your setbacks in order to move forward."

—CLIVE WOODWARD, HEAD COACH OF ENGLAND'S 2003 WORLD CUP WINNING RUGBY TEAM

Use setbacks as *springboards.*

The Three Secrets to Success

There are 3 secrets to sporting success. What do you think they are?

Secret Number 1

80% of Success is Turning Up to Practices and Matches

Obvious! But not everyone gets it. You have to put the work in if you want to improve your skills.

How good are you at turning up—at the moment? You can always get better.

Tick the box that applies to you.

❑ Not very good

❑ Some of the time

❑ Half the time

❑ Most of the time

❑ All the time

> **Remember, unless you turn up, nothing happens.**

"Turning up" also means:

✦ having your mind in gear,

✦ switched on, ready,

✦ focused on the job.

✦ Doing your best to follow the coach's instructions.

✦ Putting effort and energy into the practices.

✦ Aware of what is going on around you.

✦ Involving yourself fully in the game.

How "switched on" are you?

Tick the box that applies to you.

❑ Not very often

❑ Some of the time

❑ Half the time

❑ Lots of the time

❑ Almost always

Secret Number 2

Practice, Practice and More Practice! We only get better with Practice.

Research suggests some champions may have clocked up as many as 10,000 hours of quality practice. *Yes, 10,000 hours* by the time they are champions.

Get 1% better each time you practise and it all adds up. Steady progress gets you there—one practice at a time.

How many times a week do you do some practice? It could be with the team, or on your own.

Circle the one that applies.

Once?

Twice?

Three times?

More?

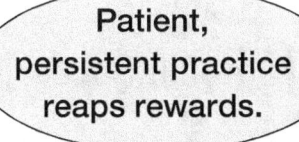

Patient, persistent practice reaps rewards.

Thoughts on Practice from Three Legends

Tennis Champion Martina Navratilova

Speaking about when she was a young player, Martina Navratilova says,

> *"There was never a day when I didn't want to play ... you know I've never seen the ball come over the net the same way twice. There's always something different about each moment, so it keeps you coming back."*

Martina won 18 Grand Slam singles titles and 6 Wimbledon Tennis titles in a row. She won singles and doubles titles at 80 tournaments.

Football (Soccer) Great Eric Cantona

When he arrived at Manchester United, Eric Cantona surprised everyone with his commitment to practice. He went a step further than everyone else, staying behind and continuing to practise after the formal practice had finished. Others began to join him.

This is what his manager, Alex Ferguson, says about him:

"... he had a crucial impact on our successes ... but nothing he did in matches meant more than the way he opened my eyes to the indispensability of practice. Practice makes players."

And now a story that will make you smile.

Golf Champion Gary Player

Gary player was a very successful professional golfer. He won 9 major championships on the Professional Golf Association (PGA) Tour and 9 major championships on the Champions' Tour.

During one competition his ball had landed in a bunker—those large holes filled with sand and scattered around every golf course. The shot to get out of it was going to be tricky. He rehearsed his shot mentally, going through it in his mind a couple of times. He focused his mind on the ball and the stroke. He gently swung the club, and, in a spray of sand, the ball lifted into the air. It flew, hovered, came down, bounced twice and stopped half a metre short of the hole.

Gary walked on towards the green to finish the hole. As he did so, a spectator shouted:

"Hey Gary, that was a really lucky shot."

"I guess you're right," said Gary, turning to the man. "But you know, it's a funny thing. The more I practise, the better I become, and the better I become, the luckier I get."

Not luck, but practice.
How excited are you about practice?

Tough Practice

Do you want to make practice even more effective? Here's how:

Stretch yourself by making your practice a bit harder than what you will meet in a match.

Then playing in a match will feel easier.

For example, you could:

+ Play against people who are older, or bigger, or stronger, or more skilful than you.

+ Play football/soccer in a small, crowded area— like a playground—to practise and improve your ball control.

What could you do in your sport?

Put a suggestion in the box:

```
┌─────────────────────────────────────────┐
│                                         │
│                                         │
│                                         │
│                                         │
│                                         │
└─────────────────────────────────────────┘
```

Words from a Winner

Boris Becker won the Wimbledon Tennis Championships at the age of 17—yes, 17! He went on to become the World Number 1 and to become Grand Slam Champion six times.

In a radio interview he talked about what helped him on the way to becoming a champion. One of them was having "humility", which he describes as:

" … the willingness to listen to your coaches,
to take advice and to test new possibilities.
To admit that you don't know everything.
Because 'Feedback is the breakfast of champions.'"

Receiving feedback means listening to comments about what's going well and what's not going so well in your game—thinking about them, then acting on them.

Another "winner", Liverpool and England footballer Steven Gerrard, says something very similar:

> *"It tells you a lot about young lads at the*
> *club when you see how they react ... I'd say*
> *the ones who listen, like I did, are the ones*
> *who take the advice and tips on board, giving*
> *themselves a better chance of succeeding."*

In a 17-year career, Steven Gerard played 709 games for Liverpool and scored 186 goals, winning 2 FA Cups, 3 League cups and 1 UEFA Champions League. He played 114 games for England, including 3 European Championships and 3 World Cups.

Secret Number 3

Calm Is Power

Calm and Focused is **Super Power**. When you are Calm and Focused, you are Relaxed and Controlled.

Your Attention is on what is Important at this Moment.

And the secret to being calm and relaxed and focused is ...? Your *breathing*. So, turn the page.

Just Breathe

We think that action is power.

But ...

Deliberately being still and focusing on your breath will calm you, refresh you and give you energy.

> So ... pause for a moment ...
> and take a breath or two.

That will get you ready to play your best.

Of course, you are breathing all the time, but this is a little different.

Try all of these ways of breathing and see which you prefer.

> Guess what? You get better
> with ... *Practice!*

Calm, Relaxed and Focused Breathing

Sit for a minute and try out these breathing exercises. After a little practice you'll be able to do them anywhere and anytime you need to.

Lengthening Your Out Breath

Breathe in through your nose to a steady count of 3.

Then breathe out of your nose to a steady count of 4.

Flower and Candle Breathing

Breathe in through your nose to a steady count of 3, pretending you are smelling a flower.

Breathe out through your mouth to a steady count of 4, pretending you are gently blowing out a candle.

Tummy Breathing

Put your hands on your stomach (just above your tummy button) and feel it expand like a balloon, as you breathe in slowly and deeply through your nose. Hold your breath while you count to two, smiling as you do so. Breathe out with a deep, slow breath.

Hand Breathing

Hold one of your hands so fingers are pointing towards the sky. Spread your fingers.

Using the first finger of your other hand and, as you *breathe in,* run that finger up your thumb. As you *breathe out,* run that finger down your thumb. Continue doing this up and down all the fingers of this hand. Do the same thing as you run your finger up and down, back towards your thumb. You can repeat the exercise using your other hand.

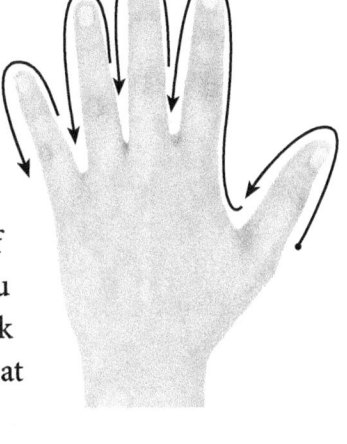

Tick or highlight the appropriate box to answer these questions.

Which do you find easiest to do?

Lengthening my out breath	Flower and Candle Breathing	Tummy Breathing	Hand Breathing

Which needs more practice?

Lengthening my out breath	Flower and Candle Breathing	Tummy Breathing	Hand Breathing

Which helps you most to be calm, relaxed and focused?

Lengthening my out breath	Flower and Candle Breathing	Tummy Breathing	Hand Breathing

Self-talk

Have you noticed that we talk to ourselves in our heads? We all do it. It's called "self-talk".

We do it to remind ourselves what to do and how to do it.

Sometimes we beat ourselves up, particularly if we have made a mistake, and it doesn't make us feel very good.

So, when something doesn't go right, be kind to yourself. Say encouraging things. We all make mistakes. It's called *being human.* Say things like, "Next time I'll relax, focus and get it right … I'm doing fine … I'm OK as I am."

Think of three more positive things you can say to yourself to be encouraging. Write them in the boxes below.

1.	2.	3.

Adding to Your Growth Mindset

Positive self-talk is part of building your Growth Mindset. What do you think of the suggestions below? Which of them would you like to say to yourself?

Circle or highlight the ones you like and that you think will help you most.

I can learn from this

I like a challenge

I'll keep going though I find it hard

I'm up for this

I'm getting there

I know what to do

I'm doing fine

Well done, me!

You Could Use a Mantra

But what's a mantra?

It's a word or phrase you repeat silently to yourself. It helps you concentrate and reminds you how you want to be.

Josh Kerr is a Scottish middle-distance runner. He won a gold medal in the 3000m race at the World Athletics Indoor Championships in March 2024. This is what he said after the race:

> *"I had to be really calm early on because it's 15 laps. And, if my heart rate is racing when I walk out, it's difficult to hold on to for a while. But I tried to keep a calm head, keep the heart rate low and just make strong, smart decisions. I had lots of mantras today, but the biggest one was just staying calm, and if I trust my instinct I am going to make good decisions."*

You can use the word *calm* like Josh did, or *breathe* as a mantra to help you to be relaxed and focused. Whatever suits you and whatever suits the situation.

What other words might *you* find useful as a mantra?

Write some on the page below. Add more as you think of them.

1. _____

2. _____

3. _____

4. _____

5. _____

6. _____

7. _____

8. _____

9. _____

10. _____

Head Up—Head Down

Keeping Your Focus on the Game

Try it now. Walk round with your head up. After a few steps, walk with your head down. Do that a few times and notice the difference.

Have you noticed where your attention is when your head is up? And when your head is down?

When your head was up, you probably found that you were looking ahead and all around you. Noticing things. Ready for action.

What happened when your head was down? Did you notice that your attention went "inside"?

When our attention is inside our heads we start to think, to remember, to notice how we feel.

Think about what that means for playing your sport. When your head is up, you are looking around you, seeing what is happening. You notice where your opponent is on the court, or where your teammates are on the pitch. You know where the ball is. You are involved in the game.

Because your head is up, you are there in the present moment and you can respond to the game and play your part.

When your head is down, you are not present. You are somewhere else. And, when does your head go down in a game? Yes, when you have lost a point, or the opposition have scored.

Then the negative thinking and the negative self-talk starts: "Oh dear, we're losing, and things are going wrong again. It happened like this last time. They're too good for us", and so on.

So, when things go against you, immediately lift your head. Choose a word that you can say to yourself that reminds you to look up—"crossbar", "basket", "umpire", "spectators"... You could even shout it aloud to remind the rest of the team!

> **Winners always hold their heads high—even before they have won.**

... and

keep your head up and your wits about you when you have just won a point or scored a goal, because:

> *"The most dangerous part of any game is when you have just scored. Everyone is on a high and concentration can lapse in moments like that."*
>
> —STEVEN GERRARD, LIVERPOOL F.C.
> AND ENGLAND INTERNATIONAL

Mind Warm-up

You can use the power of your imagination and positive self-talk to "warm-up" your mind, just like you do a warm-up for your body. You can encourage yourself and prepare yourself to be in the right state of mind to play.

You just need to sit and breathe (see pages 24–25) for a few moments and use your imagination.

> After a few breaths,
> allow your eyes to close.
> Go back in your mind ...
> to a time when you played well ...
> when the game flowed easily.
> Perhaps focus on a particular game ...
> Remember what it felt like to play well ...
> Bring back what you saw ...
> what you heard ... how you felt ...
> and feel it all again now.
> Enjoy the positive feelings ...
> Take a relaxed breath or two ...
> You are now ready for action.

The first few times you do this, it helps to have someone read this to you. Or record it on your phone and play it back.

Three Last Winning Hints

1. When you are training or practising, take it seriously. Concentrate. Focus. Put in the effort. You will reap the rewards. Keep the chat and the laughter to the minimum—save it till after the session. Because, as legendary UCLA basketball coach John Wooden put it:

"How you practise is how you play."

2. Respect your opponent(s). Play what is in front of you. Not their reputation, whether good or bad. And not what may have happened last time. A point emphasised by Chelsea F.C. and Czech Republic goalkeeper Peter Čech.

"As a player you only concentrate
on what is in front of you."

3. Use the magic of the word "YET". Remember, we learn through practice. We all have things we can't do, or can't do as well as we'd like to. So, when you think, or say, "I can't do that," add the word "YET"—and it changes everything: *"I'm not very good at ... (Whatever it is) ... YET."* It means that, with practice, you will achieve what you want to achieve.

Are you having fun?

If you find yourself not enjoying your sport, stop and think about what is happening.

If it's not fun, then something is wrong. Sport is meant to be fun—even when it's serious. Whether it's training or a match.

It may be because of something outside your control, like the weather, or other players not taking it seriously. It might be because you are tired, or not feeling very well.

It might be because you are beating yourself up too much—remember, "positive self-talk".

But it might just be because you are *trying too hard*. Expecting too much of yourself. Being too critical of your performances. And that leads to tension and tightness in the body and in the mind.

You guessed it! To relax your body and mind.

What is the way to release all this tension?

How?

Sit down and *breathe,* of course.
Put a smile on your face.
Do your favourite breathing exercise.

And then ...

To relax your body even more,
sit or lie down ...
allow your eyelids to relax and soften ...
allow your jaw to relax ...
allow your shoulders ... arms ...
and legs to become floppy.

*Even a few minutes spent like this
will refresh you.*

It's always good to "take time out" and to come back feeling
stronger and ready to play again.

To Summarize...

Here's a summary of what you are working on.

✦ Turning up—mind switched on.

✦ Listening to the coach.

✦ Fully aware of what is going on.

✦ Head up.

✦ Taking part—mind on the job.

✦ Responding positively to feedback.

✦ Building a "Growth Mindset" by developing a "can do" attitude.

✦ Encouraging yourself with positive self-talk.

✦ Picking yourself up and dusting yourself down.

✦ Challenging yourself with tougher practice.

✦ Learning to be calm, relaxed and focused.

✦ Using breathing and relaxation to be in the best frame of mind and body to play your sport.

And to HAVE FUN!

How are you doing?

To keep track of your progress, you can use this chart, or design one for yourself to put on your wall. Use it to either record training sessions, games, or both.

Put the date and **T** for *Training* or **G** for *Game* in the first box. Score each of the other boxes 1–5. 5 = high score, 1 = low score. N/A means not done.

I've filled one in as an example.

"Do something every day to raise your game."

Date T/G	Turning Up	Focused	Tough Practice	Calm & Relaxed	Breath Exercise	Positive Self-talk	Growth Mindset	Fun	Mind Warm-up
13 Oct 2023 T	5	4	N/A	3	3	4	4	4	N/A

Notes and References

Frontispiece: Vince Lombardi was a legendary American football coach best known for his nine seasons as head coach of the Green Bay Packers during the 1960s. He led them to five NFL championships and two Super Bowl wins.

Foreword: Paul Lake played for Manchester City FC and the England Under 21 side. Injury interrupted a promising career. His autobiography *I'm Not Really Here* (2011, Random House) was a *Sunday Times* best seller and the 2011 Football Book of the Year at the British Sports Book Awards. He is currently a Player Care Consultant for the Premier League and a qualified Psychotherapeutic Counsellor.

Sports beginning with "X" and "Z". Did you get any? "X" is a bit tricky. I didn't get an actual sport beginning with "X", but the letter "X" is very useful in another way. It is often put before another word to mean "Cross", as in X-Country Running or X-Country Skiing.

"Z" was too tricky, and I had to consult the internet. Did you? I found a game called Zorb. It's a strange kind of football (soccer). The players are each inside a very large inflatable bubble as they kick the ball around!

See page 45 for a full list of sports. You may have found others. One or two are a bit unusual—like Unicycle Basketball

The Boy, The Mole, the Fox and the Horse by Charlie Mackesy (Ebury Press, 2019) is a story about kindness, fear, love and friendship—and cake. It has beautiful drawings and is an enjoyable read for children and adults—but you have got to be OK with reading handwriting style print.

The song "Pick Yourself Up" was composed in 1936 by Jerome Kern and the lyrics (words) were written by Dorothy Fields. It was a long time ago but it is still good advice.

The idea of a "growth mindset" comes from the work of psychologist Carol Dweck. Through her observation and research, she discovered that our attitude and the effort we put in are what help us to get better at anything—sport, schoolwork, playing a musical instrument. We can all improve if we are up for facing the challenges we meet—and don't put limits on ourselves. If you are willing to stick to things and stretch yourself, to try new ways of doing things, to ask for help when you need it, you have a "growth mindset."

The opposite of a "growth mindset" is a "fixed mindset". Put simply, with a "fixed mindset" you believe that your abilities are fixed and there are some things you'll never be any good at, however hard you try.

Adults might like to look at: *Mindset: The New Psychology of Success.* Carol S. Dweck, Random House, 2006.

Mindset: Changing The Way You Think to Fulfil Your Potential. Carol S. Dweck, Constable and Robinson, 2012.

What it Takes: My Playbook on Life and Leadership. Sarina Wiegman, Harper Collins, 2023.

Winning! Clive Woodward, Hodder & Stoughton, 2004.

10,000 hours. In his book *Outliers: The Story of Success* (Little, Brown & Co 2008), Malcolm Gladwell looked at the ways in which successful people achieved their success, including sports people. He found that those who became very good at what they did, had all spent lots of time practising. What is important is that their practice was what you might call "good practice"—that is, deliberate, precise practice, often guided by their coach or teacher. In that way any "bad practice"—mistakes and inaccuracies—could be quickly corrected and the most effective ways to do things were stored in their minds and bodies.

On the Secret of Becoming a Legend. Martina Navratilova interview with Joe Buck, YouTube Audiorama, 8 November 2023.

Managing My Life—My Autobiography. Alex Ferguson with Hugh McIlvanney, Coronet Books Hodder & Stoughton, 2000.

Gary Player story told in *The Magic of Metaphor—77 Stories for Teachers, Trainers & Thinkers,* Nick Owen. Crown House Publishing, 2001. Primary source: Peter Connolly.

Tough practice: Basketball legend Michael Jordan was noted for making practice sessions tough for himself and for having a very full daily training schedule. He'd start the day with fellow athletes as early as 5am. They called themselves *The Breakfast Club.* Interestingly, Michael Jordan said: "(The) Breakfast Club was a mindset more than a workout. We wanted to be more prepared than anyone else". (Training to Win Like Mike—air. jordan.com)

Notice what he said: the session at The Breakfast Club "was a mindset more than a workout". In other words, it was helping to build his "growth mindset".

Jordan's preparation also included making the practice situation harder than he was likely to meet in a competitive game. The story is that he would get defenders to crowd him, jostle him and stop him from scoring in ways that would not be allowed in a game. If he could still score when it was as hard as this, then he could get through the defence in a game.

Boris Becker story told in *The Magic of Metaphor—77 Stories for Teachers, Trainers & Thinkers.* Nick Owen, Crown House Publishing, 2001. A reconstructed sports radio interview with Boris Becker.

My Liverpool Story. Steven Gerrard (with Paul Joyce), Headline Publishing 2012.

Josh Kerr interviewed by James Reid in *The i newspaper,* 4 March 2024. Josh also won a gold medal at the 2023 World Championships and a silver at the 2024 Olympics. Both of these were in the 1500m.

My Liverpool Story. Steven Gerrard (with Paul Joyce), Headline Publishing 2012.

Wooden On Leadership. John Wooden and Steve Jamison, McGraw Hill, 2005.

Interview with Peter Čech in the *Guardian Newspaper,* 15 May 2010.

An alphabetical list of sports. How many did you get?

Athletics/Archery

Basketball/Boxing/ Badminton/Bowls

Cricket/Croquet/ Canoeing

Dodge Ball/Diving

Equestrian

Football/Fell Running

Golf/Gymnastics/ Gaelic Football

Hockey/Hurling

Ice Hockey

Judo

Karate

Lacrosse

Marathon Running

Netball

Orienteering

Polo

Quoits

Rugby/Rock Climbing

Soccer/Swimming/ Skiing/Skateboarding

Tennis/Trampolining/ Table Tennis

Unicycle Basketball

Volleyball

Water Polo/Wrestling

X (See note p. 41)

Yachting

Z (See note p. 41)

Although you may well have a favourite sport—
one that you are particularly good at—
have a go at other sports. Join in and enjoy them.
There's always something to learn—
about taking part, about the mental game,
about yourself.

It also stops you taking your favourite sport
too seriously, too soon—and perhaps
falling out of love with it.

Acknowledgements

Grace Perrow and Taylor Williams for being the inspiration for writing this book.

Dave Williams for keeping me in touch with sport all these years.

Alex Dawson, Louisa Smith and Tricia Chaplin for their comments and observations.

Rosa and Rowan Bainbridge and Vicki Dawson for reading and commenting on the draft script.

Darius Omid for creating Niki.

Jonathan Lloyd for his friendship and wisdom.

My wife, Jan Williams, for all her love and support.

Richard Lyntton at richardlynttonbooks.com for all his encouragement, support and practical help.

Crown House Publishing for permission to use an extract from the interview with Boris Becker and the story about Gary Player.

Paul Lake for his supportive and positive Foreword.

About the Author

Chris Dawson BA, MSc (Ed. Management),
D. Hyp., Diploma in PE from Loughborough College
(1st Class Hons.)

Chris has been helping children, young people and adults to fulfil their potential for over fifty years. Initially this was as a schoolteacher and then as a senior manager in high schools in England—more recently as a therapist and performance coach.

He taught physical education in secondary schools and coached rugby, cricket, gymnastics and swimming. He is a qualified hypnotherapist and has qualifications in counselling and mindfulness.

Chris has five adult children and two of his sporty grandchildren, Grace and Taylor, are his inspiration for this series of books.

He lives with his wife, Jan, in Stockport, Greater Manchester, England and supports Stockport County Football Club.